YOUR FACE MY FLAG

ALSO BY JULIAN GEWIRTZ

Never Turn Back: China and the Forbidden History of the 1980s

Unlikely Partners: Chinese Reformers, Western Economists, and the Making of Global China

YOUR FACE MY FLAG
POEMS
JULIAN GEWIRTZ

COPPER CANYON PRESS
PORT TOWNSEND, WASHINGTON

Cover art: Edward Burtynsky, *Xiaolangdi Dam #4, Yellow River, Henan Province, China*, 2011. Courtesy of Robert Koch Gallery, San Francisco / Nicholas Metivier Gallery, Toronto.

Copper Canyon Press is in residence at Fort Worden State Park in Port Townsend, Washington, under the auspices of Centrum. Centrum is a gathering place for artists and creative thinkers from around the world, students of all ages and backgrounds, and audiences seeking extraordinary cultural enrichment.

LIBRARY OF CONGRESS CATALOGING-IN-PUBLICATION DATA

Names: Gewirtz, Julian B., 1989- author.
Title: Your face my flag / Julian Gewirtz.
Description: Port Townsend, Washington : Copper Canyon
Press, [2022] |
    Summary: "A collection of poems by Julian Gewirtz"
    — Provided by publisher.
Identifiers: LCCN 2022017868 (print) |
    LCCN 2022017869 (ebook) |
    ISBN 9781556596469 (paperback) |
    ISBN 9781619322653 (epub)
Subjects: LCGFT: Poetry.
Classification: LCC PS3607.E924 Y68 2022 (print) |
    LCC PS3607.E924 (ebook) |
    DDC 811/.6—dc23/eng/20220419
LC record available at https://lccn.loc.gov/2022017868
LC ebook record available at https://lccn.loc.gov/2022017869

98765432 FIRST PRINTING

COPPER CANYON PRESS
Post Office Box 271
Port Townsend, Washington 98368

www.coppercanyonpress.org

CONTENTS

YOUR FACE MY FLAG

TIME DIFFERENCE

At Final Destination, 11:06 p.m.

My new country says drinks are cheap and I know what he wants.

Bartender folds her forefinger *nine* ninety

for two, about eleven dollars. Now my country's

walking out and in the courtyard at least a hundred men

standing around shouting over music the jangle of Beijing

even hidden away, even at Destination. But I whisper

softly into his ear. Hold his hands wide. One

little kiss on each cheek or full on the mouth. Trace of my

L'Oréal. In the medieval poems *he* and *she* are not distinguished

and I see our faces everywhere, in a scroll's landscape

left blank where the figure's eyes fall, in a bowl

of half-eaten peaches, a cut sleeve, any sleeping body

turned away from view. In this corner of the end

three men gather around a fourth, face on

the ground mouth agape drooling sick

or is it pleasure—that scent of tobacco smog dirt—

Tell me what you want, night.

Stick to the wall like a damp cotton shirt. Tell me

what you want. I can talk fast or slow. I can recount

the first time we met, centuries ago, minutes ago.

I can stand still. I can recite to you any

law you want. I can say it

with passion, the end, listen, it sounds like absolutely nothing.

Arrival at Container Port, Est. 1842

What are you after,
cumulus homing in
this one afternoon

in the old treaty port—
Guangzhou, cargoes
Audi Tesla Rolex

Hermès—I won't ask you
to give me thoughts
of me, just this

portable colony's
cardboard skin
where it's torn into

and taped up. A guard
walks below the
flags on the gangway. Do

you detect—smell—this
fishless water, floes
of styrofoam thrown

overboard and my
hair black like a
screen turned off

and that smooth—
will you touch it again,
your finger unlocking

home screen this far
from home, any
translators, middlemen

like us hungering down
between the high containers,
protocols, secret treaties

every stinging night—
its dark locks thick
from the scalp of the day

shorn off after only
six hours. That's dawn.

After the One-Day Trial, January 2014

1

Drought in the inner plains.

Sandstorm shuts down the city.

Water out from the tap red.

You're my brother now
you say in the room near the university.

Nineteen in Beijing.
Already have a brother I reply.

You're sitting on my twin bed
shoulders up against the cinderblock.

Now you have two
you say smiling standing

and from my window I watch you go
through the metal gate.

Looking back up you wave twice.

Alone in my room four years later I stand
reading on my phone: *you*

have accused me

of disrupting public order.
Activities that constitute disruption of

order.

Outside snow coming down
everywhere and in the small distance

between window and streetlamp
wet blurry empty

you speak for ten minutes
till the judge cuts you off

can't hear the timbre of
your voice anymore

fear for your face your features
your quiet your open mouth odorless. Open.

•

Find a photo on my hard drive. You're holding a book of philosophy, my young face is grinning, and I remember a sentence I underlined: *Now the police dreams that one look at the gigantic map on the office wall should suffice at any given moment to establish who is related to whom and in what degree of intimacy.* Your name unprintable your face unprintable. Censor, from Latin, "to appraise, value, judge." I am always free to leave.

•

Citizenship begins with the individual, through small acts so you wrote

thousands of letters—

we had exchanged a thousand words

at most. I wrote it all down.

As much as I could. Am free to.

Wrote thousands of letters.

Thousands of leaves blowing, rusted wind,

Gobi-sweeping thirst. Thousands.

Thousands of letters coming out of the prison
and my letter, this letter, not going in.

2

Drought in the inner plains.
Sandstorm shuts down the city,

water comes out from the tap red
and you bring me a beer to drink,

cold is the shoulder of air brushing past
outside to the metal gate,

my hand on dusty honeysuckle,
no moon in the sky.

Your face my flag, your face at half-mast.

•

I meet your wife at the west gate of campus. We drink coffee and she asks
if I'm writing about you, *To him* I say, and she just nods, her head heavy
from grief, its dailyness. *My child has just been born. My family needs me. I
yearn to be there by their side. But we cannot escape politics, we can only work
to change it.* The weight of her head on her neck. *Truly, politics affects each
one of us intimately.* The pain of her small shoulders.

•

To use a man for his shadow
is to make a thing of him.

The next morning craving
I buy a ticket to Inner Mongolia.

Eight hours by bus, passing low buildings,
lampposts, then clouds, deer, grain.

To use a man for his shadow
is to make a thing of him,

a frontier, a red riverbed—
still a little water oozing through—

To use a man to use seven men
on the bus rattling softly

down the dirt road, deadnettle flowering,

shrikes ornamenting horizon, small
shadows moving fast. No rain.

To use a man for his shadow
is to make a thing of him.

•

It's just a field. An empty field.
Is it as gentle as it seems?

With each stride whispering *earth*.
Is it as gentle as it seems.

Two deer rumor in the sumac,
you know what to do.

Their bodies fling up,
you know what to do.

My want not odorless—my want a
sticky fistful of red grain—
smell of money of

coins on hands of
old bills, stink of not having it,

sun overhead casting no shade.

To use a man for his shadow
is to make a thing of him.

And if he is only shadow?

On hot days I watch
in the far shed men boil cane

steam rising sweet and I go
to them, I drink it,

fresh hot sugar
burns in my throat,
that's not pain.

I wake up in a field of dry sorghum
reddish stalks like rusted blades

and unseen at its center
a free house—for just us—

3

Weiquan lawyers (or rights protection lawyers) are a small but influential movement. They face considerable personal, financial, and professional risks. Notable Weiquan lawyers include He Weifang and Xu Zhiyong and Teng Biao and Guo Feixiong and Chen Guangcheng and Gao Zhisheng and Zheng Enchong and Xu Zhiyong Xu Zhiyong Xu Zhiyong and Li Heping and _____ *and* _____ *and* _____ *and*

•

When I wake up it's still
afternoon.

A switch flicks. Dusk
comes on quick. Automatic.

I walk
along a low wall down to the bridge

black river running loudly
like a heater turned too high

shudder shudder
shudder shudder shudder

I left that country too

shudder shudder shudder

Lightweight and unbreakable,
the moon there is dented.

Cover it with a blue cloth
before sleep, this means *come*

dreamspeech, courtroom, jailhouse bed . . .
Into separate worlds

come a stone thrown into a deep hollow
a line blotted out

what I never said to you in
the sandstorm—

your heart small and pale
in the distant night of your chest.

Prisoner of the State

A classified post-Tiananmen directive in 1989 provided instruc-
tions on how to censor former General Secretary Zhao Ziyang,
who had been placed under house arrest. No new books were
permitted, and any existing biographies were to "be destroyed."
Books and magazines "would no longer publish photographs of
Comrade Zhao Ziyang . . . and reprinted or republished books
will remove photographs of him."

After the massacre after the purge after
formalities someone took

the photograph. It is April 11.
It is timestamped 1990 into

into the negative of you
by the flowering pear tree *we came*

too late hair gone white those
first ten months at Number 6

Wealth and Power Street each petal
a fallen flag *that night of gunfire*

petal-blank your name struck out

timestamped into negative

eleventh of April, eleventh
of April, flowering gunfire every last flag—

Spend

seven years inside no visitors and four hours traveling north for one
hour per month with him no more no

                                       phone calls four men watching always
just not the man you want   Last fall the fruit trees in the courtyard refused
to ripen—*In her verses there are no sounds none*—Spend a month between
chair and bed without sleep then

                                two three four five catch
the infection from that skinny guard now it won't shake—*in my eyes
he has always been and will always be an awkward diligent poet*—That summer of
crackdown nearly thirty years ago I

                          bought a bag of apples
one's malformed tumorous a second head almost a second whole self
inside pushing out skin bulging near breaking—

                            Travel four hours north
for one hour per month with him no more. Never. Four men watching always
just not the man you want.

for Liu Xia and Liu Xiaobo

To X

(Written on This Device You Made)

> *On the last day of September, a 24-year-old migrant worker . . .*
> *jumped out of a window of a residential dormitory run by his*
> *employer, Foxconn, the huge electronics manufacturing compa-*
> *ny with a million-strong workforce that makes the majority of*
> *the world's Apple iPhones.*
>
> *The Washington Post*

1

Pick it up.
Black glass our mirror when it's
off but it is never
off. Press home button
now. Flex. Press.
My fingerprint my hot oils is that
your finger pressing the button into place now on
assembly line in Shenzhen
before it's wiped clean
I see you I think I
see you load your
poem onto it, into me, into me now *Did you, just like that, standing,*
fall asleep Did you fall farther than you meant Did you
mean me to be reading this *I want*
to touch the sky / feel that blueness so light
but I can't do
any of this / so I'm
leaving this
world / I was fine
when I came / and fine when I

left In this blue touchlight
fine rain starts
scrolling down

2

On the contract, there are four options. Two show you will consent and two show you will not. Do not tick the options that indicate you are not willing. Tick the two that say you are. If you tick the boxes that say you are not willing, the form will be cancelled.

3

What do you see? Under
razorbright lights
blue hats blue jackets
every identification card
taken away long ago you
came 28 hours by bus

Rules are: no long nails
no yawning no sitting
on the floor no talking
or walking quickly no being
late no transients or preteens
no families *If you doze off*

and fall against the machines and
there is a live wire no one will
save you The workshop
still as a ravine in autumn
When you slump and slide
back off your stool it's
a hare breaking out of the
underbrush

4

Workers have up to ten minutes for visits to the toilet Such visits are possible only if a supervisor is available and willing to stand in for the workers on the shop floor The toilets are equipped with cameras When a worker's time is up a loudspeaker calls for him by name until he returns He returns For now

5

That night rain's pouring into
                              the underpass
fills up to the brim—cup of opaque
liquid crystal display—frame—shield—

If you get lost in the city you will be
replaced *I have people lined up to*
replace you $1.85 per hour no errors

Now you turn your head to see
                              the train coming
Rain torn by wind, unstoppable rain, fetid rain
It's scentless They rinse your uniform so many times
                              it's scentless

6

I pick it up. I ask who made you *I don't understand*
                              Who was the person
who put this phone together *Do you mean call history* Was it wiped

at the factory or after how many hands touched it before mine *I don't
know myself but I can find out* I breathe in it's your air

7

Motherboard left
your village you
miss her free
garden of plums
ravenala *a language*
of tightening
screws Do you type
your poems into it

lychee   verbena   bougainvillea
eucalyptus   asbestosflower

at least three screens
a minute at least
twelve hours a day
spray the polish
onto the display
then wipe it dry
if you leave a trace
wipe it again

ten more nets go up

8

The delegation comes to visit the factory the city government seeds the clouds to cause rain it rains it clears the smog it leaves behind blue skies from the ground silver iodide rockets fly up into the clouds which condense which fall toward earth: raindrops. The air tastes harder. The light sleeker. A frozen glass is rinsed in milk.

9

Eighteen your name meaning Walk Forward

triple-bunked twelve to a room fences ten feet
tall on the roofs
                              bedsheets full of ash
dried gum in your fingerjoints and burrs
pricking behind your right shoulder

When you place it in its box
                    do you imagine me

In the testing area the belt keeps moving never stops
halfway through the sixteen-hour shift you recall
a corner of roof where one's torn   be quick—

Eighteen your name meaning Walk Forward
Eighteen meaning unfree meaning
                    falling from a great height

10

You are the one
who installs front
camera with proximity
sensor leaning
over the factory
assembly a shadow—
sensor gains awareness
six hands later in process

but you figure out how
to turn it on early *What if*
there were a faint summons
they could feel Sensor makes
a square around your
face and focuses *A pair*
of hands gently opening
a red lacquered door

"On his rare days off Xu Lizhi likes to visit bookshops, lingering in the aisles. He frequents the factory library, and writes poems and reviews. He twice applies unsuccessfully for desk jobs—as a librarian at the factory and at his favorite Shenzhen bookstore, Youyi. When a local journalist asks him about his future, he says: our lives will become better and better."

12

I pick it up with my free hand, screenshot, Xu Lizhi, you're
standing on an overpass in Shenzhen, green plaid shirt,
your right hand holds your left forefinger,
                                                you look older than
anyone your age—light traffic below and the railing's covered
in stickers, phone numbers . . .
                                                I hold you in my hand you can't feel
proof of single status physical exam wastewater pours into the river, pay stubs
scurrying like minnows *certificate of conformity* can't be both a boy and
a worker, choose one *They've trained me to refuse to skip
work, refuse sick leave, refuse to be late, refuse to leave early—*

Shenzhen once a fishing village   children laugh dashing past
green lychee trees hulls heaped trash and scrub hills above
where now stands a bronze statue of Deng Xiaoping *a corridor
made of nonfiction*   When it happened no one   was there to see it

ten more nets go up

13

You are the one
who changes air

filters in the manager's
office   the yellow-

stained black-caked
filter   a seine

that catches night in itself
all night

14

I pick it up, type in your words *A screw plunges to the ground*

working overtime at night Another worker's falling asleep on the line

iron moon head jerking *It drops straight down with a faint sound that draws*

no one's attention   just like before on the same kind

of night a person—

ten more
and grates on every window

15

The boy breathing
next to you 120 mm
tweezers turning thin

fingers the smallest
parts he does by
hand always wears

gloves to touch it
until one morning he
picks it up and

types into it *My eyes are
so tired they won't open*

16

I look at it. Locked. Is there space for a distress signal if you wanted

to leave one. I switch silencer off, hit home, it gives me

only one emergency call, no private numbers, but it can take

a picture. Will record whatever I do next. *I've heard there's a time*

difference with foreign countries, here it's daytime, there it's night—

Designed by Apple in California Assembled in China Model A1549
FCC ID BCG-E2816A IC 579C-E2816A IMEI 355790070868852

17

I pick it up

forgive me

I pick it up

Aubade, as the Addressee

In my dream you are a lion shrugging,
gesture rustling into sound: *human*

and out a thin stream of tap water
poured from my measuring cup

a hand shakes holding, and the heavy
head swings up like a camera

loose on its second-most-used axis,
quick into its viewer: *human*

turning toward me over small
distances, seconds, sunrise a small

white sheet on the floor and you speak
the first words of the day to me, your voice

a shaking hand, clink of two quarters
folded in, and loosely, the cool of them,

the smell of them, can't get it out—*human*
I say in sunlight and shrug.

FROM *A SHORT HISTORY OF THE WEST*

from *A Short History of the West*

the New Millennium

Don't go near the fire-gutted palace—

it's afternoon, not yet four,
scent of burning everywhere

in the entirely new city, don't go
into that fire-gutted air outdoors,

just go to the movies. They're showing
Troy, even here almost sold out,

smoke-thick voices, dust kicked up
warm from sunlight or men's arms,

remind me, is it to Danaë
that Zeus showers himself,

that captive, that cascade of gold coins,
a jackpot, a plague—a prisoner

meaning someone who has
nowhere else to spend it.

The West's All Here

Don't sit too close, the smell
of her perfume is somehow
here still on this mondegreen
cableknit, I'm wearing it anyway

because you'd like that,
if I reminded you of her,
you'd never say. She checks out
of the Grand Hotel Nature

with the lean vacationers
all still sunning
on the whitening dock,
those white boys whose shoulders

grow more democratic with each meal
and those girls whose voices ring
blonder than half the birds here,

loud mallards buoying
the hazards of that black
water, heads gleaming
with richest green velvet

like the stair she climbs
kicked away. Oh but liberty
you know that part
of the story, you'll find it all there

a pendulum stilled,
this *I* in the marble bar
pressed against what
experts name *serpentine,*

dark green stone-scales
which Romans thought
resembled a coiled whip-
snake that could not bite

though we have been waiting ever since.

I Describe to You the Weerdinge Men

That rope a trip wire just above
your mute deserted face the grass
and written out on sheets of onionskin
light—tattooed letters twice
the paper's weight—glowing through
this story, yesterday, a forgotten evening, the relicts
reduced to a diet of willow leaves,
their particular green littering pain
everyplace as if history were a storm
bleeding ice into the air.
That rope just above the grass—
the trip wire—I know because I fell—

I Describe to You the Yde Girl

That rope? It is a breathless *yes*
fingers press into this windy
oboe our throat—one woolen
waistband slipknotted on the neck
keeps you warm below twelve feet
of peat, lineless, a convalescent's skin
only mud the doctors dig into
unearthing each indivisible number.
How unlike the bark of this beetled elm,
its jagged beams and flagging crown
fine as the hair of a queen anemic—
hissing to be mistreated—this caused my beauty—

from *A Short History of the West*

after Master of Anthony of Burgundy's
Le Bal des Ardents *(c. 1470)*

Believing myself made of glass
I Sun King   in time of war   for fear

of shattering completely
allowed no one's touch
to touch me   how it sounds now

when I say it is not how it felt

•

Last winter you see
a suite of six courtiers

and the sweetest one   dance *en masque*
as beasts sprang from the brush,
gowns of linen soaked with resin

lined with flax, broad shoulders bare,
their twelve legs chained together

now shriek and leap   *en masque*
You see the long handsome arm,
the one arm that toward himself
topples a torch   almost inevitably

his smoke has the sweetest scent.

•

Quatorze they call me, Sun, beloved, mad,
I found a new one I want for mine,

a continent, seized
in August   *When the wind is southerly . . .*

What remains after a year of rot?
Always the pit, never the peach.

I wouldn't wish it on anyone.
To become, overnight, a *survivor*—

1680, New Territories

On the first night
the iconodule was my husband
and his estuary flesh
along my spine and voice

of my sacrum, holy
bone holding together
pelvis and mouth
opens to let in air,

no prayer, I chose you
because it is right to
not care but to own so long as
the river brims

with loess and glares,
the sun bloody hot,
and fish can't swim any way
but belly up—

we are cruel as ashes.
I chose you because
it is right not to trawl

so long as you won't
care for whatever might
be found in the net
raw and trembling—

on the first night
the new world was my husband
and his mouth flesh
along my spine toward

my nape, like
a surgeon specializing in
the removal of voice.

By the time we wake up
our wedding bed is big as
this mastodon alone on snow

plains swept with a hundred hands
lumbering away its limbs
and fur and our numberless years
together   I choose

you because the idea
of choice blows harder now and colder—

one thing's for certain,
I know what pleases you—

clocks, silks, prickly gorse,
the bitterness of chokecherries—

and every time I
return home, I bring
the cold in on my clothes.

Everyone who loves me
begs me not to do
the dangerous thing.

Only you would let me.

And the cold came in on my clothes.

from *A Short History of the West*

after Canova's Psyche Revived by Cupid's Kiss *(1793)*

1

To the god. Tonight
there are no visitors.

Storm clouds rise
over the near mountains, beyond

the finch-dense forest.
For nine and ninefold nights

I have waited
in darkness, lulled

only by wind-whine—
unmoving, bedded

muddle and buzz
into body, from between

teeth seeps forth
a strange issue

and small untouchable
sores collapse open

skin-strata, shallow
basins, suppurated

sediment. I
survey the subsidence,

does blood slow
and flow around my core?

The blighting
tendons. Slough

of river, place where flow
fallows—have I fallen?

My knees draw close
and fold. My legs

lapse. I will not leave.

    •

Bright: a begonia blooms. Yolky calyx whorls
below the twisted stigmas. Petalless yellow: the sepals.

    •

A task:
           Disorder
of grain-sand and light.
The love-wind, careless,

carrying a little chaff
and seed, lifting what is
too heavy. It comes

to pass. Day
plunges into the far massif,
where I was and was,

flail's whining
unsettles the shells,
vans of air holding

the color of your hair,
husk gray. I was given
no tools. Raised my hands
to let your name rise . . .

From height-
over-the-mountain shadows,
the winds startle cool

eddies, dry-spooled air
unweaving the grain,

hazed rain clouds
follow the crossing
currents, streaming
from the sky's raised face—

Were you there? Resting
on the low hay-bed,
looking toward me as I left

as a last breeze lazed
the wooden hold in
the granary.
What remains is only

cold and golden.

2

The second task:
To winnow thin
sticks from the sharp-sliver
arrows. Fine fingerwork
by feel to find
the breaking down
of browns. Were I
an arrow: freed
from the bowstring
to become vector—no,
quivered into one thing.

·

As a pulley shakes
when rope runs
through it,

the bushes
new-bloomed, shivering,
opening the meadows

dowered with trees—
heavy-leaved, hovering
above, and the silent

star-pulses, alive.
Spring crawls into
eyes and scratches

its way out—
When he comes,
I almost do not

notice his light
arrival, low
breeze-blow,

the feathered air
suspending him
above me—

when he is not
here, it is as if

he is not here.

Of Discovery: A Letter

This swarm is breaking the sunrise

into dirty emeralds, morning-shard

flashed quick off tiny wings—

one's bruiting about in my overcoat,

threadbare it kept me cold

all fall, patchy

holes like yellow tormentil

tangled and dead in the pasture.

Always two children bargaining

loudly now in the hallway.

Last night I rested my head

on a new pillow and this morning

I am walking all the way out

to the far tree where I met you.

The first button's done wrong.

You never get the rest right.

Social Studies

In May the men who carve eggshells
do a mean business, meaning

their hands work ceaseless and along
the sidewalks creased with pollen
they walk home southward through

tonight's gloom and batting
its inky robe. It's dry cotton
hemmed with a line of *inclement*—
when what's to come is merciless.

I know you think inclement means
incoming, forecast storm may never come,

a ground-sunk heat, like weights laid
on a scale kept in imperfect balance,
uneasy left plate floating lower

and you spend all afternoon trying
to make it even with every bronze
dreidel laid out in front of you

and I know, I know you spend whole days at home,
school's cancelled for inclement weather,
sky's all albumen, yolkless . . .
I know you loved robins best.

In May the men who carve eggshells
do a mean business, meaning

the finished shell may be
an unlightable lantern—or a birdcage—

or even a spring—helical hollow
coiled emptied-out egg
pressed lightly between fingers—

Arm'd and Fearless

Out fast from that first city
this boy born under the sign of the swan
runs due north along a line of spoonwoods.

Leave behind your queen-sized bed,
silk pajamas, orchid, symbols,

and I the voice mumble *magnolia*
into *no* that air *no*

Come back to me sweet blue one
if I still flute song if it's not gone

how can I say anything else?
           Broken kylix,

bowl with no horizontals,
husk: lean back. What's two soft
hands emptying from its clay lip.

And I will be the painter chosen
to adorn the bottom of the cup:

my work invisible so long as
the cup is full.

from *A Short History of the West*

For a long time the sky's polluted white
is a sheet pulled over my head

now a memoir of rain is falling
unclear gray pellets, dust,
I remember—*petrichor*—

my Greek teacher's breath
on my ear explaining
how to give the scent of fresh
water on rock a name

but the stench of low tide's
what reminds me of him

     •

now the sea is extending
its long arm across the territory

no gulls no single sheet
in the unhalting match-blind wind

THE DREAM OF POSSESSION

Not about Love

Someday the scientists will devise

a way for me to hold

you without even needing

to walk across the room.

It will take practice.

The empire of discipline,

cold and heavy. Empire

of the unnaturally clean,

fluorescent night, an engine

starting in the distance.

Far off in the distance.

Own Weather

> *In 2025 US aerospace forces can "own the weather." ... From enhancing friendly operations or disrupting those of the enemy via small-scale tailoring of natural weather patterns to complete dominance of global communications and counterspace control, weather-modification offers the war fighter a wide range of possible options.*
>
> US Department of the Air Force,
> Weather as a Force Multiplier (1996)

1

No breeze, no music,
here late in the progress
of the day. Indifferent

day. Sparrow fretting for
rain gathers grass and
seeds. Sparrow just

a spindly shape leaving

now as the unseasonable
cold front moves in low

the air show above the parade

last Independence Day

those sharp-nosed fighters—

that day I read a story
about cloud-seeding

an experiment they call
selective precipitation modification

how a drone disperses carbon dust in

air above lake to soak up sun

hotter vapor rises condenses

and falls as rain—falls
as not-rain—*This delivery*

method could also be used for precipitation suppression To deny fresh water or induce drought It offers tools to shape the battlespace in ways never before possible The tremendous capabilities that could result from this field are ignored at our own peril It is pertinent to all possible futures

2

That day I read it I
unread it trying to
push it back under
as a man dumping dirt

on new-bloomed phlox
sees it's too
pink to hide pink's
in his mind now

impertinent pink

—can't focus on
that tall one's
skinny shoulders

cold copper wire
almost blue and
possessed of

inner weather
inner resources
the first ancient
poem a prayer

for rain not love—
let go of your
climate down into

this ending now
badwind gusting
fast off the mountains

damp and angry
against the grass
against my face

3

Or look away from your page your trees don't

follow the line your curiosity stops there at sky

white as a placebo   numb as a missile

also distant also entirely yours and you didn't make it

even breaking dissembling disassembling sky

crack of lightning bone-hot your *complete*

dominance—yielding if you say so—if

describe—if *dream of possession*—

4

Some segments of society will always be ~~reluctant to examine controversial issues such as weather-modification~~ *dividing and indifferent blue*

5

A car engine a driver

in sunglasses another
man handsome looks at

me *lonely cloud* when
I do not move or

speak he does not stop

6

The last poem   an order for drought

7

Now even the centers
of the trees stir

a bird a common
whitethroat lets out

its high robotic call
(a tape fast-forwarding
through a love song)

and looks at me and
leaves. I almost feel

not yet. This rain
will be heavy as
(I will be still as)

the body of a wounded
soldier on his back
at Austerlitz

All is falsehood

Except that infinite sky

All is falsehood

8

Except that infinite sky

9

Still no rain.
How little time

passes this way.
That sparrow

is back already
gathering
building

just like before.
It should

know better

not yet.

Incomplete List of Unequal Treaties

The "unequal treaties," a series of agreements in which China was forced to concede many of its territorial and sovereignty rights to foreign imperialist powers . . . form the foundation of the Chinese Communist Party's campaign of "patriotic education."

1. Treaty of Nanjing, 1842

    . . . being desirous of putting an end to the existing misunderstandings;

2. Treaty of the Bogue, 1843

4. Treaty of Wanghia, 1844

    . . . for peace, amity, and commerce, with tariff of duties;

6. Treaty of Canton, 1847

    . . . wishing to reestablish and ameliorate the former relations of friendship and commerce;

11. Treaty of Kulja, 1851

    (in Russian, French, and Manchu, no Chinese text)

18. Treaty of Tianjin, 1858

    . . . desiring to maintain firm, lasting, and sincere friendship;

    (four thousand men, three full days of burning)

25. Treaty of Shimonoseki, 1895

    . . . cedes to Japan in perpetuity;

    (so I did to others what had been done to me)

28. Boxer Protocol, 1901

    . . . the conditions laid down . . . accepted in their entirety;

(continued below)

Reading at the Window

(The Golden Age of Time)

> The river's belly
> rubs against the rocks
> without sensation,
> an unceasing,
> all hunger *to capture*
> *on a surface*
> *a great range of*
> *knowledge about*
> *the world* and
> what this river does is
> not devour but
> carry—soil—wind
> loosening the coils of
> silt, soft mica, pits
> of quartz, bone—
> paint loess-yellow,
> sometimes whiter
> spots scarring
> the borders between
> goods, hands, republics,
> *a tendency to regard*
> *paintings as windows opening*
> *directly onto another*
> *time and place* slightly
> out of focus and glinting,
> tower blocks below the
> newbuild, engravable,
> lip curves of an
> atlas opened

to a place I left still willing to return

                              and turning
                              the heavy pages
                              of this *Art*

of the Golden Age at last I find
the young woman reading a letter
at an open window, her lover
half a world away, foot soldier
in the colonial trade, whole body
facing letter, street, town square,
then out further the eight-lane bridge
stinking of exhaust, twenty million
lives inside city limits—and yet here
now on her table the wide-lipped
bowl of peaches, apples, plums overturning,
did she get up quickly yes getting
up closer to the windowlight from
that world outside where she isn't,
but the bowl from Jingdezhen
this fruit spills out of
is the dark where my eyes go—
porcelain bowl knocked ajar
barely visible in that same shadow

                              just then, just
                              then in time

sold into this history.

Hardcore Innocence in Hangzhou

We've been reading dirty
books, the kind with scurf
in their spines, cracking
their backs over my bed

flakes onto my pillow
but we can't stop yet,
I've recently learned
this halo around the moon

is just more water
frozen into jewels so
small they don't fall
toward us. Tonight's forecast

is heavy snow.
Kingdom, you learned early
the blank law of attraction
Like likes Like

yet you may not have noticed
the kink of future I pressed
into your pocket watch,
long hand locketed down

now it's always
a few minutes before midnight—
we can have a drink
on the house.

The planes can see us,
listen, wind droning the
organ of these elms,

grass's unsteady metronome.
We're stumbling drunk,
too fumbling to touch

the garden's succulents
swollen beyond recognition . . .
Am I *you*? These colors
of night, stiff-scented, freezing—
And if I want you, that doesn't

make you want me.

A Being within an Envelope

(George Staunton)

In the imperial
planetarium
the bodiless voice
lilts like a zazou suit,
oversized shoulders
too loud for any
song to play under—

The stars come out tonight
or is it the satellites.
Comets streak through
this dark like spit

and in a room
just like this one
someone is teaching
someone to do it
as if pursed
lips could make
the strange new language

pool. I can walk slowly
past a tall candle
and the flame
will not shiver.

Until silence
comes over the screen,
lightbulbs dizzy on
slowly across the ceiling
and the audience

begins to stir and
it's a day with two dawns,
the only applause a fistful of aubades.

I have not finished
what I came here to do.

Western Sketches

1. Teen Idyll

Your voice is the coven nesting
in the shroud of a summer
spruce. Now I find some part

of you there in that town
where the manufacture
of locks long ago fell away
for the blowing of lipped glass.

What a dirty smile the beach is.

And these birds dizzying up one by one by
one, almost like cloudy droplets
lifting from that bay

after a week without distances.
In the harbor two small boats
punch into weathered water, midnight

risen up these concrete walls
cragged, bits of green glass, slick pearls
of clear glass, and iron scraps,

a century's deadbolts thrown into
what is not exactly stone

and over the clouds billows of purple
blush like a sleeve in Pontormo

who is famed for what he let float

away into the bare arms of the day.

2. Absent in the Spring

That one's some El Greco blond
spandrel cornice all arms
of blue into our late modern light

scoundrel of clouds hotter
than green stones of the city at noon
and sun's now gone down now drawn down

and white's a shock on the clouds—intruding—
looking at you from across
the street in a crowd packed with dry colors
swirling dust in sunlight—

and here still as if we had not left at all—never
left—not Toledo—a lifetime of watching

trees fraying into thick brushes
on a hundred canvases a hundred pigments
of a hundred compositions now hummed
as sloped sounds and a few are swimming back . . .

The clouds. The glare. Elsewhere a meadow
river. Shallow water flowing ahead. Threaded
with tassels scattered into the grasses. And
minnows moving over the bottom quick

also as shadows. And you go back into your crowd.

3. Shelter in Place

You must pull down the book of perfect beauties

its heavy slug of dead rabbit, pollen
smeared on the nose, cracking as it opens
each sheet's stale air and musts up

touching that tight-woven gray
smoothest of all the underbelly colors
kept close to the ground when the thing is alive

and what now. There's history on the loose,
I shutter my green window. And my red
window. That tree outside doesn't stop the wind

from shaking the three or four rocks in its sack
as if it actually wants us to open up.
We know better. I think it's nowhere

near here now, though it might have passed through,
it's no Billy the Kid, not so fine for eyes
to riddle, these hills to fold open for, and elsewhere

that still life hangs with its gamey russets,
lamed faces nailed—I loved just once letting it
wander the mansion of my name.

4. The Bliss of Solitude

In my left hand you were a burning rope.

All day long this air was thin as the smile
of quartered mangoes or the glow
of skin in my nightlight—

And all day long I was speaking
in the perpetually blue field
past tall wheat to the sycamore tree

I remember climbing up hollering
as the sky filled from the top with that dark
sinking like cold smoke into the city . . .

Tonight the meadow is laughing again
while a kit of jacobins mulls
in wire cages sleeping inside the fantails

of their collars and in that garden
an old man in his green silk pajamas stitched
with fishermen angling silver rivers

wraps his arms around the moonlight
falling on a thin wool blanket—
waxing moon, half-weighted hammock.

5. Travelers Returned

Hills like peaches sliced open and bright

steaming, the hot insides of carcasses
exposed to air. The land below us black as
a sky until the constellations of the city

broke through faint and we descended
toward that blind galaxy on the valley floor.
Just a week ago today we walked past archaic

torsos where marble floors wing up
the scent of warm milk but this air is cold,
a gloom of manure tracing the rim

of the lagoon, that tongue-pink reef
jagged as a kiss caught on teeth,
salt in the mouth, salt in the eyes, your hand—

molten dribble still hissing life into the islands
though they are dark and dead. Even now. Torches

hooked that horizon together at sunset once—

Excavation

1

The boy who wears a feather in his ear
is not like a bird sitting by the river,

his dark head in the lap of this other.

Both of them have strangely soft hair.

The black-haired boy's shoulders
are broad from a summer's work

back home in _____. His long hair
covers his eyes. His legs are thick

with muscle, the bounce and verve of the soccer ball,
and he smells like a field of pepper, a cedar tree

fallen into a stream and stripped. The other boy
wears a plaid bathing suit. He is entirely dry.

The beard he grew on vacation
hangs from his face. There is red moss

on the pale stones. He sits, his thin shoulders
float unsteadily, off-center but balanced,

like the top bar of a mobile. He usually holds
his hands as if he is just about to rub dirt from them.

But here his fingers, two fingers, are knuckle-deep
in the silk of dark hair, and two more against

the warm forehead, hard of skull, and his thumb
thrown up, flung into air touching nothing, a gesture

to beckon who back in?

2

The boy wears a feather in his ear.
It dangles from a brassy hook, it marks

him as Figure A in the scene set beside
the river he watches the sun rise across

each morning, the scene I'm watching,
feather like a leaf in eddy of air,

like a scrap of bay horse's hide
warm as grass through dry dirt,

and now the fingers of Figure A fly up,
press to his ear, what does he hear I cannot

hear—can he? And how did he
become the one whose name I recall,

fingers pressing beneath
his arms and the haunt of him

everywhere on them, and now he's playing
with grass, pulling at it, and quickly

all the leaves go quiet at their edges
as Figure B enters the scene

a step ahead of the shadows,
as Figure A greets him with

his whole body turned upward, something like a hand
held out to be taken, a hand held and shaken,

spotted feather playing in wind
casting shadows on his neck on the lips

of Figure B against the neck of Figure A
distorted over the muscles of their necks,

sky streaked all sinewy with day and their faces
a day just beginning, no proof

of the earring's weight anymore,
fingers touching the back of Figure A

like lost tourists wandering past
the silent man in the afternoon air

sitting out front at a tea house watching
the centuries' disoriented sightseers.

He can't hear everything they're saying.
He decides at last not to get up

not to speak over the sound of the river
over the slow wind in hot trees.

He gave up his wings to get arms.

3

Now I have been too long looking at him.
Too long thinking about him

and he's been picking at
the skin around his nails, barbs angled

away, stinging, as the persimmons
ripen after a day in air, hanging from hooks

in a shop's open window, object
entirely fragrance, entirely the object's

breaking-down in sun, a boy running
upper limbs held wide through a wet field

of wheat and for a week the smell of wheat
dimpled into him. I'll give you a hint.

It all comes to me like seashells
from someone else's travels, always

the sense of overhearing ocean, whirring
of blood, same blood beating for . . .

Once he found him underfoot, a toy

on the playroom floor, something to make
a body jump back, cry out. Take note.

When a boy, I had a plastic castle.
I filled it with bright figures.

Notes

"At Final Destination" refers to the nightclub Destination 目的地 in Beijing. It draws on Bret Hinsch's *Passions of the Cut Sleeve: The Male Homosexual Tradition in China.*

"Arrival at Container Port, Est. 1842" draws on Stephen R. Platt's *Imperial Twilight: The Opium War and the End of China's Last Golden Age.*

"After the One-Day Trial, January 2014" adapts language from Chinese lawyer Xu Zhiyong's testimony, delivered at his trial on January 22, 2014; he was sentenced to four years in prison, released in July 2017, and imprisoned again in February 2020. The italicized sentence "Now the police dreams . . ." is quoted from Hannah Arendt's *The Origins of Totalitarianism.* The definition of the Weiquan movement is a pastiche of encyclopedia sources.

"Prisoner of the State" takes its title from the posthumously published memoirs of former Chinese Communist Party General Secretary Zhao Ziyang.

"To X (Written on This Device You Made)" responds to the collection *Iron Moon: An Anthology of Chinese Worker Poetry* (ed. Qin Xiaoyu, trans. Eleanor Goodman). It adapts language from Chinese and English media reports, including a *Time* magazine article by Emily Rauhala, on the suicides at the Foxconn facilities in mainland China where iPhones are assembled.

"I Describe to You the Weerdinge Men" and "I Describe to You the Yde Girl" refer to bog bodies displayed at the Drents Museum in the Netherlands.

"from *A Short History of the West*" (2) refers to the French monarchs Louis XIV and Charles VI and uses a phrase from *Hamlet.*

"1680, New Territories" is in memory of Lucie Brock-Broido (1956–2018).

"Arm'd and Fearless" takes its title from a phrase in Walt Whitman's "We two boys together clinging" in *Leaves of Grass*.

"Not about Love" takes its title from Fiona Apple's song of the same name.

"Own Weather" draws on a public report produced by the U.S. Department of the Air Force, *Weather as a Force Multiplier: Owning the Weather in 2025* (1996). It uses phrases from John Berryman, William Wordsworth, and Wallace Stevens, as well as a passage from Leo Tolstoy's *War and Peace* also quoted in Samuel Moyn's *Humane: How the United States Abandoned Peace and Reinvented War*.

"Incomplete List of Unequal Treaties" draws on text from the treaties listed.

"Reading at the Window (The Golden Age of Time)" refers to Johannes Vermeer's *Girl Reading a Letter at an Open Window* and adapts language from essays on Vermeer by the scholars Svetlana Alpers and Timothy Brook, as well as Elizabeth Bishop's poem "Over 2,000 Illustrations and a Complete Concordance."

"Hardcore Innocence in Hangzhou" is in memory of Sandy McClatchy (1945–2018). Its title is taken from a phrase in Alan Hollinghurst's chapbook of poems, *Confidential Chats with Boys,* published while he was a graduate student at Oxford University.

"A Being within an Envelope (George Stanton)" refers to the figure of George Staunton, who had begun to study the Chinese language as a child and at age twelve traveled as a member of Lord Macartney's unsuccessful mission to the imperial Qing court.

"Absent in the Spring" takes its title from a phrase in Shakespeare's Sonnet 98 and refers to El Greco's *View of Toledo.*

"The Bliss of Solitude" takes its title from a phrase in William Wordsworth's "I Wandered Lonely as a Cloud" and refers to Zha Shibiao's Qing Dynasty scroll painting *Old Man Boating on a River.*

"Excavation" takes its title from Willem de Kooning's painting of the same name.

Acknowledgments

I extend my thanks to the editors of the following publications in which these poems previously appeared, sometimes in different forms: *The Adroit Journal, AGNI, Boston Review, Colorado Review, Conjunctions, Denver Quarterly, Harvard Review, HIV Here & Now,* Lambda Literary, *Nat. Brut, The Nation, The New Republic, The Oxonian Review,* PEN America, *Ploughshares, West Branch,* and *The Yale Review,* as well as the anthologies *Best New Poets 2016* (selected by Mary Szybist) and *Best American Poetry 2020* (selected by Paisley Rekdal). Harvard University, Columbia University, the Rhodes Trust, the Council on Foreign Relations, and the Academy of American Poets provided support that enabled the writing of these poems.

I am grateful to so many people who helped me find my way in poetry. To my teachers Lucie Brock-Broido, gone too soon; Joanna Klink, guide in my first workshop; Renée Harlow and Christiane Jacox, earliest poet-teachers I knew; and especially Jorie Graham, without whom these poems, and this book, would not exist. To those who encouraged, taught, and inspired me at crucial moments, including Bennet Bergman, Chen Qiufan, Christina Davis, Christopher Alessandrini, D.A. Powell, David Wallace, Erica McAlpine, Hannah Sullivan, Hao Jingfang, Henri Cole, Hugh Foley, J.D. McClatchy, Jane Miller, Jonathan Galassi, Josh Aiken, Julian Lucas, Kaleem Hawa, Kristie La, Margaret Ross, Matt Aucoin, Matthew Bevis, Max Ritvo, Moira Weigel, Monica Youn, Peter Sacks, Rachel Kolb, Richie Hofmann, Sarah Howe, Spencer Reece, Susan Bianconi, Timothy Donnelly, Trisha Baga, Xiaolu Guo, Yuan Yang, and workshop companions, including Amanda Auerbach, Amanda Gunn, Angelo Mao, Adrienne Raphel, Charlotte Lieberman, Chris Spaide, Kate Monaghan, Laura Kolbe, Lisa Hiton, and Michael Weinstein. To Molly Dektar and to Zoe Hitzig. To Fareed. To my brother, Alec, and our parents.

Finally, my deep gratitude goes to Michael Wiegers, John Pierce, Claretta Holsey, Marisa Vito, Ryo Yamaguchi, the publishing interns, and everyone at Copper Canyon Press who helped bring this book into the world.

About the Author

Julian Gewirtz is a poet and historian. His poems have appeared in *Best American Poetry, Boston Review,* Lambda Literary, *The Nation, The New Republic,* PEN America, *Ploughshares, The Yale Review,* and elsewhere. He is also the author of two books on the history of modern China, *Never Turn Back: China and the Forbidden History of the 1980s,* which Minxin Pei called "the definitive book on China in the 1980s," and *Unlikely Partners: Chinese Reformers, Western Economists, and the Making of Global China,* which *The Economist* described as "a gripping read." He co-edited an issue of *Logic Magazine* on China and technology and has written essays and reviews for *The New York Times, The Guardian, Harper's, Foreign Affairs, Prac Crit,* and *Parnassus: Poetry in Review.* He previously served in the Obama administration and has been Senior Fellow for China Studies at the Council on Foreign Relations, an Academy Scholar at Harvard's Weatherhead Center for International Affairs, and a lecturer in history at Harvard University and Columbia University.

Poetry is vital to language and living. Since 1972, Copper Canyon Press has published extraordinary poetry from around the world to engage the imaginations and intellects of readers, writers, booksellers, librarians, teachers, students, and donors.

COPPER CANYON PRESS WISHES TO EXTEND A SPECIAL THANKS TO THE FOLLOWING SUPPORTERS WHO PROVIDED FUNDING DURING THE COVID-19 PANDEMIC:

Academy of American Poets (Literary Relief Fund)
City of Seattle Office of Arts & Culture
Community of Literary Magazines and Presses (Literary Relief Fund)
Economic Development Council of Jefferson County
4Culture
National Book Foundation (Literary Relief Fund)
Poetry Foundation
U.S. Department of the Treasury Payroll Protection Program

WE ARE GRATEFUL FOR THE MAJOR SUPPORT PROVIDED BY:

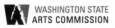

TO LEARN MORE ABOUT UNDERWRITING
COPPER CANYON PRESS TITLES,
PLEASE CALL 360-385-4925 EXT. 103

WE ARE GRATEFUL FOR THE MAJOR SUPPORT
PROVIDED BY:

Richard Andrews
Anonymous (3)
Jill Baker and Jeffrey Bishop
Anne and Geoffrey Barker
In honor of Ida Bauer, Betsy
 Gifford, and Beverly Sachar
Donna Bellew
Matthew Bellew
Sarah Bird
Will Blythe
John Branch
Diana Broze
John R. Cahill
Sarah Cavanaugh
Stephanie Ellis-Smith and
 Douglas Smith
Austin Evans
Saramel Evans
Mimi Gardner Gates
Gull Industries Inc. on behalf of
 William True
The Trust of Warren A. Gummow
William R. Hearst III
Carolyn and Robert Hedin
David and Jane Hibbard
Bruce Kahn
Phil Kovacevich and Eric Wechsler

Lakeside Industries Inc. on behalf
 of Jeanne Marie Lee
Maureen Lee and Mark Busto
Peter Lewis and Johnna Turiano
Ellie Mathews and Carl Youngmann
 as The North Press
Larry Mawby and Lois Bahle
Hank and Liesel Meijer
Jack Nicholson
Gregg Orr
Petunia Charitable Fund and
 adviser Elizabeth Hebert
Suzanne Rapp and Mark Hamilton
Adam and Lynn Rauch
Emily and Dan Raymond
Joseph C. Roberts
Jill and Bill Ruckelshaus
Cynthia Sears
Kim and Jeff Seely
Joan F. Woods
Barbara and Charles Wright
In honor of C.D. Wright,
 from Forrest Gander
Caleb Young as C. Young Creative
The dedicated interns and
 faithful volunteers of
 Copper Canyon Press

The Chinese character for poetry is made up of two parts:
"word" and "temple." It also serves as pressmark for
Copper Canyon Press.

The poems are set in Arno Pro.
Book design and composition by Phil Kovacevich.